whitewards

THE SLOVAK LIST

Katarína Kucbelová

whitewards

Translated by Julia and Peter Sherwood

LONDON NEW YORK CALCUTTA

Slovenské
literárne
centrum

This book was published with the financial support of the SLOLIA Board, The Slovak Literary Centre.

THE SLOVAK LIST
Series Editor: Julia Sherwood

Seagull Books, 2025

First published in Slovak as *k bielej*
Original Slovak text © Katarína Kucbelová

First published in English translation
by Seagull Books, 2025
English translation © Julia and Peter Sherwood, 2025

ISBN 978 1 80309 563 9

British Library Cataloguing-in-Publication Data
A catalogue record for this book is available
from the British Library

Typeset by Seagull Books, Calcutta, India
Printed and bound by Hyam Enterprises, Calcutta, India

contents

everything is as it used to be everything is as it used to be everything is as it used to be

a foreword

Let me begin with a personal experience—or rather, a confession. I acquainted myself with the works of Katarína Kucbelová during my university years, determined to devour as much contemporary and classic poetry as humanly possible. I read her first three book-length poems or compositions—*Duály* (Duals, 2003), *Šport* (Sport, 2006) and *Malé veľké mesto* (Little Big City, 2008)—as well as her then-just-published *Vie, čo urobí* (*Knowing What to Do*, 2013) in chronological order. At the time, I was buried under an avalanche of compulsory reading from the Slovak literary canon, and emerged with only a faint notion of what I had read. But the primal tension remained—a gut feeling that beneath the seemingly cold, remote non-verse was something of utmost importance, something that drew me back to Kucbelová's works without an iota of resistance.

Over time, I began to see her books as texts that blur the boundary between conventional and unconventional poetic writing—labyrinthine works demanding both analytical precision and rational interpretation to unveil a stunning portrait of human emotionality and a profound engagement with the elusive questions of life. As poetry is wont to do.

Now for some indisputable facts. This fifth book of poetry by Kucbelová, *whitewards*, appeared after a nine-year hiatus from the genre. It provoked strongly polarized critical responses and garnered three literary awards in 2023: the Zlatá vlna, the Václav Burian Prize and the Tatra Banka Foundation Award for Arts. In the meantime, Kucbelová also published two works of prose: *Čepiec* (*The Bonnet*, 2019; English translation by Julia and Peter Sherwood published by Seagull Books in 2024) and *Modroslepost'* (Chasing Blue, 2023). These writings also demonstrate her distinct methodical, multifocal observations of the world.

This may sound subjective, slippery, open to challenge. So let us examine more thoroughly what Kucbelová's poetry entails. Her books rest on the premise that the world is ambiguous and can be observed in a plethora of ways. They stage a tension between the irrational, subjective, individualist and corporeal experiences—and the objective, factual, law-bound order of the world. That rift is often their central focus, recurring across a variety of topics.

Like all her work, *whitewards* offers an idiosyncratic approach to storytelling: events are suggested but not fixed, characters are shadowy, setting and time are rendered as abstract concepts. We are never sure what the figures are doing, where they are headed, what performance they are watching, or why a woman has awakened from a deep slumber. We do not know where these events are taking place, or when. We are merely observing fragments that speak little for themselves, but they unsettle and pose the questions: Is anything we see or perceive meaningful, relevant, or even real? What lies beyond these glimpses, these views and panoramas? How credible are these representations? How reliable is language itself, when words contradict the reality they name, when the grammar of a sentence subverts the speaker's intent? Who is speaking—and why?

Such line of questioning is not accidental. After all, *whitewards* leans into them. It revels in uncertainty, abstraction and a distrust of the bond between language and the world it claims to describe. This intensifies the cavalcade of questions and relentless quarrels with the world around it.

Questioning—without the expectation of definitive or satisfactory answers—is one of Kucbelová's strategies for interrogating language and its users. Across the book, a multiplicity of characters, speakers, voices and subjects emerge, sometimes as persons, sometimes in the form of an undefined collective. Modalities shift, illocutionary acts multiply, even languages morph and interlace. English surfaces as a hollow lingua franca, a collective, amorphous language stripped of meaning except as ritual or façade—a language of alienation and illusion. It becomes a chorus, an echo of familiar phrases: mantras we chant to reassure ourselves that the world is in order. Idioms and collocations with long-lost meanings. Proper names that feel unmoored from context. In this respect, *whitewards* is an anxious exploration of language's ever-loosening tie to reality and to the materiality of the world.

Kucbelová frequently tackles this growing detachment from natural, lived experience. In w*hitewards*, it reaches a kind of peak. In poem 11, the possibility of poetic expression is itself cast into doubt—every interpretation of the world is revealed as highly subjective and projective. In the end, all that is aesthetic, axiological and emotional—the entire complexity of lived experience—amounts to a gaze into a blank page, a pristine canvas, a white hillside.

Superficially, white—and its myriad forms and cultural connotations—sits at the heart of the matter. A glance through any Western dictionary of symbols will suggest that white stands for purity, perfection, happiness, beginnings, unity, innocence. But in many non-Western cultures, it is associated with the opposite: white signals the underworld, death, sorrow and mourning, the end, spirits, ancestors. Kucbelová brings these meanings together. In the scene with three figures on a white hillside, introduced in the opening poem, nothing remains stable: not the number of figures, nor the significance of white, nor even the scene's claim to reality. The monochromatic palette hints at the interplay of light and shadow. In symbolic terms, light represents the deity, creation, elimination of darkness, knowledge, ethereality, life, fortune, elevation; while shadow suggests manifestation, the underlying phenomena, vitality, the putativeness of the world, the inner essence, the soul. Kucbelová accentuates white as a paradox, capable of evoking purity and order, as well as annihilation and void.

This crumbling begins immediately: the snow with three figures transforms into dry grass illuminated by the sun. Many such descriptions feel like paintings, stylized moments suspended in time and space. Poem 31 even invokes painting with lead white—the whitest of whites—with all its toxicity and metaphysical baggage. Poem 39 offers another near-perfect white, extracted from the mineral barytes, which in Slovak fittingly carries the name *ťaživec*, which can mean 'burden', both literal, a heavy stone, or metaphorical, a mental burden. Yet another white, lowly in comparison with the others, appears as *blanc de blancs*, a champagne, trivialized into a symbol of consumerist oblivion—luxury amid the disintegration of the natural order of the world.

White is both the beginning and the end, a serpent devouring its tail. The story starts with an image and unravels into uncertainty. It ends with a crash—headfirst into a blinding white barrier, perhaps plasterboard—or an indeterminate world 'beyond'—a closing question: *is this how it was meant to be*? What follows is a blank page, a white space.

The original book cover mirrors this. At first glance, it's a minimalist sunlit forest: strokes and splashes of black. But over time—after reading—the cover is no longer 'white'. It's marked: smudged, fingerprinted, touched.

Leaving a permanent mark—contamination, desecration, irreversible transformation—these motifs appear throughout the book, especially in relation to ecological concerns. This reflects the broader arc of Kucbelová's oeuvre: the tension between a desire for stasis and life's inevitable dynamism. *Duály* mapped this tension onto relationships, *Šport* onto bodily life, *Malé veľké mesto* onto time and space, *Vie, čo urobí* onto social and environmental realities. In *whitewards*, it becomes a yearning for a pure, untouched world—frustrated by the impossibility of preserving it.

The poem-composition depicts the world losing shape, menaced by a vague threat.

Ecological collapse unfolds as if outside human awareness; people drift through simulated life, as if numbed and cradled into lethargy. Poem 5 states this bluntly: people saturate their world with substitutions to avoid the rumble of their bloodflow. Seasonal time dissolves; months lose their forms and connotations, as in Poem 23, and time itself frays.

Poem 12 directly addresses global warming, casting doubt on the term's meaning, the interests that lay behind its use and whether any response is still viable. Ice and snow—or their absence—depict a world that is out of order. Snow falls, but other things do as well. In poem 34, Kucbelová lists toponyms that once held poetic weight but now seem disturbingly literal—*black snow*, *black water*—supplemented with the mantra: *everything is as it used to be*. What once evoked nostalgia—Indian summer, scenic villages, a remembered home—now fades into the surreal, the sinister. A black panorama. One thinks, inevitably, of Goya's *Pinturas negras*, those dark, disturbing visions painted on the walls of his own house in his final years.

And again, interpretation delves into microscopic detail—hunting for echoes, tracing webs of connections, wandering far but always under control.

Let us now leave this subjective terrain of free-floating poetic reflection and end with a final fact: It is highly unusual for a Slovak poetry collection to appear in English translation just three years after publication.

And yet: here we are, with *whitewards* by Katarína Kucbelová, in English.

Viliam Nádaskay

w h

i t

e w

a r

d s

1.

three figures climbing
a white mountainside.

it's not snow
it's just luminous, dry grass

weight has slipped out of the body
at pace
yet remained in place

they are too far down,
she wouldn't say they're walking

she wouldn't say she's standing

can it even be called movement?

2.

the sharp tips of the pines

aren't snow
just bare wood
up high
windswept
like a giant snowflake spinning

was there no point to the past year?

a skier was almost hit
by a falling drone

a sodden branch plummeted down right
        before us
crashing on our car
the dent in the bonnet

set out at once to collect
the raindrops

a tree has collapsed into the lake
its branches frozen into the ice
a fragile coniferous alliance

how much are we not hearing?

the forest will melt
in the fog
left in the ice glowing last

are holes
roots scramble up to the surface

ferocious struggles we can't see
the snowflakes will eventually dissolve in the
    water

3.

the warming can be measured by
its scent

at twelve degrees

the unmelted remains of orientation

we sway to and fro
our heads rock

is it the wind?

a beat
only much slower

oblivious
we sway

unbuttoning
we shift from one foot to the other
getting wasted
shedding items of clothing

oblivious of each other
our bodies swaying

we could go to sleep
but might we rather stay
awake?
perhaps not numb to the bone

there's plenty of time
tomorrow will be no different
only a little hazier
the difference will be harder to detect

we sway
our bodies
in dull jerks
the tempo slow

but rhythmical
once in a while we grab hold of a branch

second by second
minute by minute

we keep tasting the wind
gaping for the snowflakes
our wounded tongues
dipping in
flickering in alarm beneath the freshly
    formed crust
the snow yielding to the pressure of the
    moist warmth

its time will come

we do it
because what else
what else can we do

with a bit of luck
we'll fall asleep

with a bit of luck
we won't melt when our eyes
beneath the surface
stop flickering and flashing
frantically
we will no longer remember

4.

three figures climbing a hill
or is it two?

has someone been lost in the light?

(is the light warm or cold?)

in the depths of the radiance
an unexpected message vibrates

(is it good news or bad?)

no, it’s not news
it’s a stray junk message

5.

we have climbed the hill
and sat on a rock

sheltering from the wind
cool, motionless and still
we have stopped breathing
becoming conscious
of our heartbeat

each of us of our own
the rush of our own blood circulating

we have turned into
remote oil platforms
huge drilling rigs

breeding grounds for thousands of
    microorganisms
gigantic holiday resorts

may you find success
may you find peace
may you find love
may you find joy

I am your home
your ecosystem
your motherland
your polis
your soil
your abode

some of you are my guests
you have come from far away
'*enjoy yourselves and have fun*'
make yourselves comfortable

a long and perilous journey lies ahead

6.

yes
home is a notion of our culture
you mustn't feel bound by our way of life
'*feel free*'

7.

hard frost and many casualties
are regularly forecast

we used to
enjoy the weather forecasts

we used to revisit the past
forgetting
the last time it was twenty below
or once even minus thirty-eight

in this very spot

we forget
but weather forecasts connect us to
past records of attempts to survive

we don't want to remember
we're not going to
we don't have to

we know, though belatedly,
that even in bad weather it's not a question of
    the right clothes
but of the right
'*outfit*'

8.

after they revived her
she was no longer
the same

she stopped seeing them
as they weren't talking to her
but rather to the person they had known

used to know

she lost the strength to meet new people

how much time has passed?
how much time would not be too long?

she wanted to

wait out a few more consecutive seasons

turning meanwhile into a person
of last resort

they were afraid of her

but they kept coming with their children
whom they couldn't handle
she had a rapport with them,
with slaves and domestic staff
with the old and disabled
sometimes lonely mothers would seek her
    out
or lonely heads of corporations
she had a rapport with all of them
she was merely there
but they said
they found answers

they spread the news, still afraid of her

some came just to tell her
things they dared not reveal to anyone else

she knew that some stories had to be told
to someone

when she didn't understand
she would ask and they would answer
that was all she did

they were afraid of her just like of their own
irreversible decisions
of their emotional investments that didn't
    pay off
of the wasted time that began to expire
while they waited
for sleep, for some order,
to land, in queues,
for a film
to end

they kept coming to see her
often telling her the same thing over and
    over

slowly she learned
that sometimes a story needs to be told
again and again
before it leaves a person
and lets them live
or die

9.

may you find success
may you find peace
may you find love
may you find joy

10.

it must have been the melted snow
which froze, then started to melt again

the trees started shedding
their mantle of ice

meekly getting ready

we are grateful for anything
we manage to glimpse
perhaps to maintain the illusion

that we will be able to act
to use our weapons

cleavers, cheese knives,
assorted graters and cutters

we don't want to end up like snowflakes

on water

11.

is it good news or bad?

will the radiance drown the good?
will the darkness engulf the bad?

is radiance a maze or a funnel?
is darkness a maze or a funnel?

will the radiance engulf the good?
will the darkness drown the bad?

will they disappear? stop? switch off?

is this how the final stage of oblivion will
look?
of being numb to the savours of nostalgia
and sorrow?

the shades of mystery and fragrance?
the sounds of restraint and excitement?
the combinations of colours of joy?
what else can we still see?

in the meantime, what are we hearing?
a vibrating escalation
of rotary cutters and saws
as they approach silently and wistfully?
as they grip noiselessly and plaintively?
as they sink in soundlessly and pleasurably?
as they sob inaudibly and abruptly?

was it a sob or a sigh?
did you hear it?

12.

we don't remember

how many seasons has this winter been
    going on?
'*oh, ages*'
excuse me?
it's been ages

when we want summer, we travel
the same with spring
some people would like to swap winter
    briefly
for autumnal leaving and forgiving
get ready again, this time more mindfully
(should we have known that?)
or go back in time and explore

let stories melt and refreeze
perhaps they have just realized a return from
    spring or summer
might be fatal

some deny
and some have stopped using

that word

they spend their time discussing more apt
    definitions
but it's just waiting for spring again
time they had to kill
doing some activity
this is how they clear up their doubts
is this temporary? is this permanent?
when it ends, will everything be as before?
as it has always been?

do we still remember?
will we have to get used to something new?

should we start now?
should we have started earlier?

new definitions are created by groups of
    people
who prefer an answer
some groups have started applying these
    definitions to themselves
others have not, though others defined them
    that way
some groups are bigger
others try to convince everyone else
still others don't want to know
some were against creating any new
    definitions
some formed alliances, others opposed
    them,
yet others said that it wasn't global
and since it wasn't global it didn't matter
it was just winter, that was all, and so on and
    so forth

sometimes we ask, is this really winter?
is this how snowflakes are meant to look?
piling up in the fold of a sleeve like
    frogspawn
they are hard to capture on camera and sting
    the face

and many, many people have left
some thought they were leaving forever
others, just for a while
others have come back and yet others have
    stayed
regardless of what they had planned

13.

but this is not what happened!
why are you telling lies?

14.

her body has become heavy, a burden
she was unable to get up

she slipped out of her body
leaving all her weight inside
bodyweight was relevant no longer
she watched it from above
instead of feeling light she got a fright
and returned

so much effort is needed to bestir
a living organism
or living organisms
here in this home, dwelling, motherland,
    polis

the weight has dissipated
in the shared movement
of bodies sliding
through frozen days
any peak will do
any kind of escape

15.

she's shouting but they are far away
they can't hear her
is this really her voice?
does she still have a voice?

16.

he holds her tight and from behind
it must be him, and his body, taller, legs
    akimbo, is in the shade
and choking her throat
his head is bent down
he is holding her hands behind her back, tied
    to her torso
she offers feeble resistance, it is a
    performance
without props or toys
the singer is around thirty
she sings of loneliness
of being misunderstood
of emptiness and the extinction of her world
as usual

as before
her singing is halting
her choking, tearful voice her only way of
    fighting
but fighting whom?

17.

yesterday it was still available
various commodities keep being
    discontinued
no matter how much we click and
    resuscitate,

let's have something else
what else could we have?

a brioche? some ramen? raki? a matcha latte?
    a ceviche?

we've been on the verge of leaving for several
    months
yet we haven't planned any trips

where else could we go?
where have we yet not been?

you mustn't feel bound by our way of life
'*feel free*'

18.

and later, discussing the concert
I said
she was wearing a dazzling white dress and
had platinum blonde hair
you disagreed
and said she wore a red dress with thin
straps
you were willing to concede that she was
blonde
I refused to accept that
adamant that the only red thing about her
were her lips

was it a show or a concert?

19.

how did we manage to survive this?
have we survived it?

20.

he is holding her by the ankle
they are lying on the ground while she is
        trying to break free

we forget
whether she was barefoot

perhaps a single
high-heeled shoe
left behind them on the stage

we won't tell each other
and will never learn
what really happened

21.

three figures lying in the snow
we don't know for how long
perhaps it isn't snow

isn't there another figure
lying there?
why aren't they moving?

what can't we see yet?

sometimes it seems that it's all over
but then the sky clouds over again
fog presses into our eyes
choosing one of us
settling under the bark and under the
fingernails

in grooves, scars and wrinkles
eventually smoothing everything out

softening everything?
no, blunting

blurring in a pretend mystery
we pretend we're waiting for a miracle
a ray from baroque clouds

it isn't fog, it's smog

22.

may you find success
may you find peace
may you find love
may you find joy

23.

a branch plummeted down in front of us
after landing, it flew up again, a violent
    flapping

we thought it was petals snowing down
but it's just snow again
can they keep trying to blossom?

you mustn't feel bound
by our notions of time

we pretend it helps

people go swimming in the frozen lake
car parks on the shores are packed
like in summer
it's August. is it August?

it's March. is it March?
it's October. is it October?

November brings a modicum of relief
November like it used to be
November like it's always been

most suicides occur in May
(hanging oneself from a cherry tree)

was there no point to the past year?
how long did it last?

icy water sears the skin

24.

people used to say
as always
now, instead of as always, they say
as it used to be

25.

is this white?
no, it’s grey

26.

sometimes people asked her
what to do

she didn't write their stories down
or tell them to anyone else
they were concealed in the questions
she asked of those
who came to see her
those were her answers

at times she would give a direct answer

I don't know

but they kept coming

after a heavy fall of snow

she was cut off
the stream of visitors ceased
and her house stayed sealed

she closed the shutters
stopped heating and eating and went to bed
in the cellar
watched as her pulse slowed down,
and the time between taking breaths grew
longer
as did the time between stories and faces

that floated in and out of her mind
until they stopped altogether

after some time she came round again

27.

the first thing she saw were three figures
climbing the slope
what is this place?
who are they?
at what point in time?
she wanted to go down to meet them

down to earth

would it be cold or warm?

did she really see them?

28.

a man tied a noose on a cherry tree
the wood was brittle
the branch snapped and he survived

29.

a heavy snowfall
isn't it just a white canvas
behind which everything is different?
it's bound to end somewhere

isn't it just a white canvas
with snow falling on it?

no, it is snowing before it and behind it

isn't it just a slow connection?
pixels alternating in shades of grey and white
behind which we cannot see?
we don't focus

30.

I'll wait until the petals of red velvet turn
 black
I'll let them fall
now
(the treacherous allure of stalks)
I'll cut them in half
then keep cutting them,
gathering everything into a neat little pile
I'll combine the petals with the stalks and
 leaves
'*enjoy your meal*'

what is all this soil for?
I'm promoting warmth
adding flowers as if stoking a hearth

I'll give it a good stir
and wait until it gives off a fresh stench
of almost total decomposition

may you find happiness
'*well done*'

can I bury my hands in it?
in this fresh soil?
or rather, my feet?
my bare feet
which are always freezing

I want to leave hot footprints
you will read them like handwriting
without a code
(we were taught only to invest and not to
    procrastinate)

'*stay safe and take care*'

31.

to achieve a dazzling whiteness
the whitest white
to touch it
immortalize it
since even the whitest snow
absorbs as much as a tenth of the light
for the colour white to be visible at all

we will warm up slabs of lead with
    horsedung
sprinkle them with vinegar
and in the steam a white flower will blossom
ceruse

the path to enlightenment and to freeing
    oneself

from dependence on instinct
leads through pain,
through cramps of the stomach and
    intestines
the painter slowly becomes paralysed
and dies of poisoning

and then the dazzling white emerges
releasing us from our weight and
    corporeality
guiding us
across times
across eras
across worlds

32.

is it revelation or clarification?
a deluge of radiance or order?

33.

they seem too small from high up
should she worry about them?
(suddenly she knew she wasn't afraid of
them)
are they fleeing or just walking?

sometimes they are so tiny she can no longer
see them
but she knows they are there
they might not be able to talk to each other
but that's no hindrance

34.

grey snow is falling
small tufts in whimsical shapes

again we have lost our bearings

is it snow or dust?

it turns into black water
as it lands

we don't find black water unsettling
haven't we always walked on black water
leaving black footprints on black pavements?

there are so many places
called

blackwater

blackwater mountain pass
everything is as it used to be

blackwater pub
everything is as it used to be

blackwater village
everything is as it used to be

blackwater stream
everything is as it used to be

blackwater lake
everything is as it used to be

blackwater street
everything is as it used to be

blackwater neighbourhood
everything is as it used to be

blackwater spring
everything is as it used to be

blackwater river
everything is as it used to be

blackwater waterfall
everything is as it used to be

blackwater strait
everything is as it used to be

blackwater saddleback
everything is as it used to be

blackwater valley
everything is as it used to be

blackwater gorge
everything is as it used to be

everything is as it was before
everything is as it used to be

everything will be as it used to be
‘*everything’s gonna be all right*’

it's actually quite romantic

it sounds like home

it reminds us of an Indian summer

and the village buried under volcanic dust
looks like a winter postcard

35.

may I?
yes, come
closer?
do come
won't I cave in?
no, keep going
are you holding me?
yes, I am
come on then
closer
closer
keep going

36.

when we were little
everyone stayed at home in bad weather
it was no time for going out

now we go out in all weathers
we sway to and fro
waiting
trembling with anticipation
there are still so many things
for us to do
for us to order
for us to try and celebrate

hydroponic screams of joy
some voices have sounded already
some scars have burst open

some wounds have hissed
some sighs have spilled
some embraces have boiled over
blanc de blancs
glasses!

37.

we sway to and fro
fall down and get up again
faint and come round again

what people remember most are beginnings
    and ends
everyone in a different way

38.

I’m scared how I’ll land
don’t worry, you won’t feel anything
but I want to

39.

someone has invented a shade of white
that reflects almost all light
absorbing less than two per cent
if you walk past
this almost perfect whiteness
you won't see it and you'll be suffused by a
    dazzling chill

the name of the mineral that produces the
    whitest white
is barytes, heavy
no need to panic
the name is derived from its density
no one said it was going to be light

in the end you yield to
temptation
and enter

crashing into a wall, of course,
like in a slapstick comedy

who is going to laugh?
will anyone laugh?

40.

where is that place?
where are you?

'play it again'

41.

you stand before the radiance
you take a step closer
your hands encounter an obstacle
you guess it's plasterboard
you break into a run
and burst through it

42.

you're lying on the ground

can you move your hand?

you move your hand
and feel the earth beneath you

you lift your head
and begin to see

from below again

43.

is this how it was meant to be?